LOST & FOUND

Robert Powell was born and raised in Ottawa, Canada, and now lives in York. He has worked for many years in the fields of journalism, photography, the arts and urbanism, and is an Honorary Fellow of the Royal Institute of British Architects.

He has published three collections of poetry, *Harvest of Light* (Stone Flower, 2007), *All* (Valley Press, 2015) and *Riverain* (Valley Press, 2018) as well as an artist's book and exhibition, *A Small Box of River* (2016) in collaboration with artist Jake Attree. He won the 2012 Elmet Prize judged by Kathleen Jamie, was commended in the 2017 National Poetry Competition, and his poems and stories have appeared in *Acumen, Dream Catcher, Orbis, The North, The Rialto*, and elsewhere in the U.K. and Canada.

In 2017, he wrote and co-produced, with Ben Pugh, *The River Speaks*, a short film funded by the Canal & River Trust 'Arts on the Waterways' programme. In 2018 he published *Aura* (AmosLAB, Abo Akademi University) as part of his residency at Saari in Finland, and in 2020 *Notes From a Border River* (AmosLAB), documenting his collaborative project on the Irish border during Brexit negotiations.

to Lin

Lost & Found

Robert Powell

with best wishes

Robert
December 2021

VP

Valley Press

First published in 2021 by Valley Press
Woodend, The Crescent, Scarborough, YO11 2PW
www.valleypressuk.com

ISBN 978-1-912436-71-2
Cat. no. VP0191

Copyright © Robert Powell 2021

The right of Robert Powell to be identified as the
author of this work has been asserted in accordance with
the Copyright, Designs and Patents Act 1988.

All rights reserved. No part of this publication may be
reproduced, stored in or introduced into a retrieval system,
or transmitted in any form, by any means (electronic,
mechanical, photocopying, recording or otherwise) without
prior written permission from the rights holders.

A CIP record for this book is available from the British Library.

Cover and text design by Peter Barnfather.
Cover photograph by Robert Powell –
'Glass Retrieved From the Aura River, 2018'.
Edited by Julia Deakin.

Printed and bound in Great Britain by
Imprint Digital, Upton Pyne, Exeter.

for Dianne

Contents

Wish 11

I. TIMES

Emergency 15
Fable 16
Times 17
Irish Ferry During Brexit Negotiations 19
L'été, 1917 20
Signed Bridge in a Field 21
Lost Ways 22
Post-Apocalypse-sur-Mer 23
Communal 24
Things to do on a sunny day, no. 15 25
Sculpting a Pebble 26
About Grief 27
The Red Ferry 28
Canadian Pacific 29
Steam Train, North Wales 30
The Winter Valley 31
'Firefighters rescue man from river' 32

2. TELLING

    Testament 37
    Derelict Cabin Guarded by a Bridge and Two Trees 38
    Bay Window 39
    Lost 42
    Early Warning 43
    Society 44
    Our Polar Bear 45
    Encounter 46
    Pond 47
    Fifteen 48
    Catalpa 49
    At the Bowling Alley 50
    The Telling 52
    Empire 54
    Migration 55

3. THE WOMAN ARE KNITING

    The Border River 59
    Walking from Ireland to Ireland 60
    The Women Are Knitting 62
    Collage 63
    Lilacs 64
    Woman on a Bridge, Ireland 65
    Garden Buddha 67
    HPA 515 68
    Journey 69
    December Wedding, 1942 70
    Catch 71
    Instructions for Counting a River 73
    The Old Ox Road by the Aura 74
    The Horses, Northern Ireland 75
    Coastal Moon 76

    Notes 79
    Acknowledgements 81

Wish

i.m. George Butterworth, composer, 1885–1916

Lift this wish from the mute dust-case of my chest,
decode the barred ink scrawl, set instruments
to its symbols – violin, cello, timpani, flute –
and players to give each tongue; unhasp
the locked halls so the living will come,
old and young, to gather in the shared
air of their breath, dance against death,
and hear again the bright song sung.

I. TIMES

Emergency

and the street is full of distant neighbours
pulled together from their night-long beds
in the morning sun standing
apart in the empty space
like actors surprised on stage
the curtain suddenly risen

in nightgowns pyjamas onesies they
greet each other as if they'd just climbed
from death so joyful it was all a dream
and now it's over they can talk freely
about what it's like in the dark
and not to be there

a boy strokes a pine-cone
a grandmother curtseys giggling
a girl on stilts sings to the sky
and a man in socks volunteers
to carry a leaf with extreme care
through the slight wind sifting the air

while others offer to take responsibility
for a dandelion a bottle top
a dead spider in a tin can
a till receipt an earthworm
a sparrow's egg a slice
of glass with the dawn still in it

and one gazes at a pebble
not a special pebble just
a common morsel of world
the world that was almost lost
the world we were losing before
we woke up
happily

Fable

Then the President asked:

*Why won't anyone
talk to me about Death?*

There was
a long silence.

I will, I said
stepping forward.

The gilded room
drained of lackeys,
bodyguards, hacks.

Then we sat alone
and he leaned close,
eyes wide,
like a child listening
to a bedtime story.

When we last saw him
silhouetted on the dawn sky,
the President was
a seething pillar
black with flies

from capital to base;
and the bitter air over our land
tasted something like hope
something like expiation
something like grief.

Times

It's the time of horse-chestnuts in the wind surging huge as cargo
    Of the search for the bankrupt banker's booty
Of dogs hunting poachers in Kruger National Park
    The time of house martins rushing willows along the Ouse
The Secretary of State making himself into a spider
    The lassoing of tigers
Elon Musk selling all his homes to fly into space
    Clean air flooding the cities
Innocent wolves returning amid a national obesity crisis
    VE Day celebrated by bees

It's the time when times appear as times within other times
    Of Josephine Baker visiting French airmen at Elvington
A bomb shelter buried since 1942 with shoes and toys
    A picture of bluebells spread like a lost lake you wanted to swim across
Of Germany's cricketers back in the crease
    Borders reunited after long periods of collective amnesia
The time of suits from Canary Wharf joining in the county line-dance
    A flute playing in the rain
When boxers will nurse the economy back to health
    And petals fall in a perfect circle as if placed by a mathematician in the night

It's the time when things both stop and continue
    The time of long walks around the living room
Of surplus electricity from wind farms
    When grief breaches suddenly inside like a whale
A time for meaningless words to become fashionable
    The time of riots of colour
When wild garlic is so perfect for adding flavour to a rack of lamb
    When the prehistoric woman's body lies in a well in some other country
Visas are only temporary lifeboats
    Caravan holidays attract a younger crowd

It's the time of empty buses carrying memory from one place to another
    A time for the President to play golf in his bunker
When the old king's crown is found dumped in a skip
    When it's not easy being a billionaire
When there are unbelievable bursts of lilac in the streets
    It's the time to Drink Pink the 30 best rosé wines
Of drive-in cinemas expecting a bumper year
    Of scientists sleep-walking in fear among silent tills
When love is found in an old drawer curled up like a necklace
    and global markets rally.

Irish Ferry During Brexit Negotiations

The ship, unstately,
seems steady,
all risks rhetorical.
Yet metal gossips,
each rivet nervous
with sea-pulse.

Spray-shot windows,
green fields of sea.
Waves purse
their slow, long lips
with a promise of light,
but drift away.

On the horizon,
a thumb-smudge of land –
Man, America, *Hy Brasil*,
republic or queendom,
one Ireland or another –
depends who's dreaming.

L'été, 1917

after Bonnard

The scene is two-thirds dizzy
with greens, blues, the brush flushing
wind through trees, thick
and swirling, left and right
like leaved flames
into the centre

where in sun-splashed
grass and furze
two naked women loll
rounded as in Rubens
or in any British high street
comparing voluptuous notes

while at the bottom of the frame,
lost in summer shadow, blue
as if underwater,
children in dresses and bows
play, doze, dream, and do
whatever children did then, or do.

And from all this you wouldn't know
there's a war on somewhere
though even in this painted place
time and perspective are being
blown apart, collapsed
into a chilled present

tense with expectation.
And is that robed figure
just now appearing
in the scarily near distance
bringing us the news
no one wants to hear?

Signed Bridge in a Field

The troll who lives under here was a man
who scribed his name in damp cement

below loud load-beams and sheet-metal
rust, then left decades past.

Now an internet of lightshadow
laps his grooved text, and there

he squats by his sculpture, letting
his hand stir the water as it passes

like that of the girl in a pale yellow dress
he watched being rowed on the same river in town

by some moustached toff in a boater
who fancied his chances long ago.

*I worked this farm for the landlord
fifty years and we laid this bridge,*

*my son and I, in 1926, a year of brute
heat. Now you can all fuck off.*

Lost Ways

Irish Border, 2019

Why were the railways
that bound us briefly
so utterly wrecked?

The ghosts of their tracks leading
to and from the smashed or renovated skulls
of little stations in important small places,
the empty bone-sockets of bridges that wedded hills,
made faced-off riverbanks converse,
now spook the lands they shrank
and span the loaded air everywhere
in the united kingdom of summer –

and here too,
in the constantly broken news,
from wind-drowned abutments
that reminisce under troubled elderflower cream
and stretch once more over border water
between Lifford and Strabane,
clearly invisible.

Post-Apocalypse-sur-Mer

after a photo of Dungeness beach by Gail Fox

After the end we did our best
with the bits that were left,
our rainbow city of junk
strewn above the tideline,
plastics mainly
(*they shall inherit…*)

Your place, my love,
a pilfered Portaloo
battered and rinsed –
mine, a rust-red container
packed once with all the tea
in China, and now just me.

On this stage
we play out what remains,
while over our progress
the passing clouds gaze down,
like Greek gods watching the races,
trying hard to keep straight faces.

Communal

for Owen

Reading through your PhD
about the many risks to middle-aged cooperatives
which *creak* and *slip* in the entrancing flux of time,
capital, and habit, I look up now and then
to flex my eyes on the wind beyond the window.

I remember you nestled in my hands at a hospital called Grace,
a creature knowing nothing but maybe sound, light and heat,
and after that in the bicycle seat behind me by the grey river, leaves
crackling under our wheels, and after that hurrying out the door on your way
to skipping your history exam, or trouble, or France.

History matters I said sternly then, as fathers will. Now here I am
brain-draining to follow your meticulous marshalling of ideas
that pass over my head like the geese above that October river.
The challenge is how a collective, or for that matter
a neighbourhood or nation, can resist *the iron rule of oligarchy*

which tempts communal effort towards profit, or hierarchy, or both.
Against this you propose *nuance*, *integration*, the continuous aspiration
to an impossible state of balance, a *Goldilocks Zone*.
Meanwhile, wind spills and thrutches in the nameless neighbours' trees,
crimson fists of rowanberries bob above the ladder that leans

on the brick wall between theirs and ours – placed, I admit,
mainly for the convenience of the cat. Everything creaks, slips, unites
with everywhere else, wind shakes the pages of leaves, summer and autumn
collude towards winter, and the ladder continues to make its offer up the wall
and over, no one climbing it these divisive days, not even the cat.

Things to do on a sunny day, no. 15

after Anthony McCall, 'Solid Light Works', 2018

Go down out of this
under the earth
meet all of the others –
whole half-remembered
bodies or just

a hand, a cheek
a turned hip
a young girl's dress
that swings briefly
out of the wall
of mist, then

back in quickly
unseen again
the air there silver
a silk vapour
the colour of shock –

and a voice says
*come back up it's sunny here
no rain forecast today
come back*, but they're
gone and you can't go

Sculpting a Pebble

for Frank Brummel

Bent over stone for hours,
the sculptor grinds
a perfect pebble –
a task normally requiring
ten thousand years,
the long tongue of a river,
a sea's agenda.

Simple, around the size
of a baby's head,
silken as the inside
of an upper arm,
it's a model of accuracy.
Next to a real one
I bet you can't tell them apart.

Two pebbles – both needing
the sun, or human touch,
for a quantum of warmth,
both losing warmth and its memory
so quickly, like the dead –
or even more keenly, perhaps,
someone the dead have left behind.

About Grief

Last night I slept with my dead friend's wife – it's OK,
we were both dead too I think, and thus irresponsible
as happens in dreams, those strange corridors
of seeing and believing. There are no rules there.
For example, the bed was unnaturally large, a bright ploughed lake,
and both of her grown-up children were kids again, worming
beneath the covers, curious about what we were up to,
which of course was nothing since we were both as still as.
I mean 'Death' – what can you say? There's sure to be a lot of stuff
that gets redacted. So just in case: I've put the antique WW I tin
with all the money onto the top of the wardrobe, which should fool
the shorter thieves at least. Thought I'd better tell someone……

and it's almost dawn, almost October. Once again objects
are finding their familiar forms, and there's first light growing
in the sky over the neighbours' ridiculously extended house,
though the windows are still dark with that particular darkness
sleeping houses have, quite different from the dark in woods at night
or caves at any time, for example. They're like eyes that are closed
yet full of memory, as if they know something we don't.
Why do people think they need so much space these days?
My friend and I spent thousands of hours together. I miss him.
I'm hoping the cat in the garden won't see me here in the window.
She'll be hungry, and possibly start to wail, disturbing everyone,
in dreams or not, still gone, still here.

The Red Ferry

Turku, Finland, 2018

On the red ferry,
shoppers, children, workers
with worries, laughter, gossip.
The ferryman looks tired.
A baby cries to the gulls.

Hauled on its chain,
busy in our busy city,
the ferry goes on its small
important journeys,
back and forth

across the water.
Night falls, and in darkness
the old church bell,
always the same,
never the same,
here to there
the black ferry rides.

My darling, why
didn't you meet me
on the other side?
You said you'd love me
forever and a day.

Canadian Pacific

for Dianne

By now like this train we've no choice where we're going –
east and away from the whale places, long raven beaches,
dominions of fir, and the Chinese-money highrises

to track a long, broad river, calm among pastures
but shredded to white when the forests close round.
There are shifting towers of mist, miles high and wide,

ahead in the dusk, clouds we ride into as rain, and the talk
among passengers passes through immigration, new hips,
cucumber seeds, and the possibility of tethering to satellites.

We stop, and night is falling. You rest on my shoulder. Beyond
my reflection in the window I count the wagons we've paused for,
freighted with stacked containers, 200 or so heading onwards

in darkness with logos like Blue Sky. They get priority, still doing
what the steel was laid here for by 19th century workers, most
imported, as it happens, from China. Some profits are visible.

Must be lots of wealth round here, you murmur,
eyes still closed, as we move on. *You never see houses,
just driveways among trees disappearing......*

Steam Train, North Wales

We're all pretending to be in love with the first half
of the 20th century. *Mobiles away, please!* cries the guard –
a friendly revenant – *they're not yet invented!*

Shushing and hissing, this serious old concatenation of metals
plays along – wheels grumble and knock, the nostalgic roof
rattles authentically. Up we go, up and out

from a slate-dark tunnel. Condensed steam clings
to the windows, smoke swirls into trees to marry mist,
red handfuls of berries float on green and grey

and the far mountains go topless. Everywhere, bales
of late August hay lie in their waiting-rooms and we climb,
all of us, steeply through bracken thick as fur,

then into huge blank spaces, high where sheep
scurry under the sky with their sad rainbow
tattoos of belonging.

Now a woman, who's been dozing throughout
in her cushion of fat, sits up suddenly. *Look!* she cries,
Somebody's thrown stone walls over the hills to hold them down!

The Winter Valley

for Colin Webster

Everywhere water raced down roots
and rock, as if panic-stricken,
late for some meeting.

In the valley we crossed soaked meadows
and stone-faced dye-work dykes,
roofless rooms into which steeps of beech
poured rinsed moor-blood clear as gin.

Behind, we saw crag-sides evaporate
to shroud-weather hulking fast towards us,
crows in its hair, but when it came its face had turned –
white, precise ice-cobs tumbled to earth like light gifts.

Around us hung a nacreous glare we couldn't read,
like revelation. Each silent branch and bird was still.
Then sky banished rain, and high on the hill,
wings unwrapped, wind became again.

'Firefighters rescue man from river'

News Item 1,103

When the news came in
we deployed our tallest ladders
to scan the horizons for fakery.
Then we looked for scapegoats.

But It was too hot for the cops,
way past boiling point
for the Water Rescue Team
(ducks on scorched wings
fish with smoke inhalation…)
too probable a pyre
even for the have-a-go-heroes.
So the job landed back on us.

Then we wondered where to put the river.
We could flood the city, blame it on the weather;
we could culvert the thing – out of sight, out of mind –
or divert its course, transform its ancient groove,
like Valencia did, into a pleasant park –
until at last a passing politician
suggested the Museum.

So in the dead of night
we unravelled our hoses,
manned the pumps,
decanted the whole stream –
all her creatures and light, currents, depths,
drink-cans, maps, snapshots, songs, lovers' trysts,
family days out, fishermen's wild tales –
into display cases packed
with the memory of river.

Finally
our bravest volunteers,
with danger money,
the highest boots,
the fewest children,
waded out through riverbed mud
towards the man drowning in fire.

2. TELLING

Testament

after a photograph of a child c. 1860

The boat I held could not
sail, and was not mine:
the clothes I wore felt odd,
and were also not mine.

The room was a glass box,
my mother had faith
in God's will. There's
an ogre with one brass eye
under a tall black hill.

And so I keep still, so still.

Derelict Cabin Guarded by a Bridge and Two Trees

Stranger, go carefully – who you know can't help you here.
Rooted to his job, this bouncer disguised as a birch
won't need to frisk you, will mimic instead the shimmer
of your heart's aura as you pass.

Next, the iron bridge drums your footfall
down into the common stream, reverbs in voices
from other times – long ago, yesterday, the last minute,
tomorrow. And a few steps on, the second guard

blocks the way utterly, storm-punched giant
from a folk-tale, beefcake arms snapped across
the path, here to tell travellers of the ogre, the witch,
the unsolvable riddle: *Little people, best not go further,*

for what happened will happen despite all beauty
and brightness under that small chimney you glimpse
past the long woodwind wreck of my falling –
a man's labours lost in a hulled room, capsized

and drifting now in waterlight amid the sweet
empty chatter of sparrows and river,
the sky loitering nearby,
just waiting to enter without asking.

Bay Window

Finland, 2018

1.

On one solitary cycle ride
a window appeared ahead,
a bright bay opening its arms
to a little beach without ambition
between the branches
of childhood.

2.

My English dentist left me a text.
When I called back, a voice said:
*We last saw you a few years ago –
are you still with us?*

No, my teeth are in Finland now,
and besides, I'm only ten –
I stand with my bike,
the circled rims of water
sliding in, and in again.

3.

As a boy, my father raced
for a club on Lake Ontario –
Singles, Doubles, War Canoe –
gave it up to work, have a family,
row himself slowly into distances
away from water.

4.

In time and space I'm far from then:
this is the Baltic, calm as a lake
in windless memory that clasps
the paintbrush reeds by their thin waists
like a crowd of ballerinas
while last year's crop lies,
a flattened horizon in the sand.

5.

My first dentist was called Wolf –
clearly a gifted man, but with a name
like that, in a country of boundless opportunity,
and considering the imaginations of children,
why choose to be a dentist?

6.

In the bay, on the sand,
a small white rowboat
hauled carefully up on land,
half full of rain,
held by a chain.

7.

One winter evening,
my father took me to the Wolf's den
on the 2nd floor of an old brick building
over a drugstore.

In fever, or just scared, my teeth
tap-danced on their enamel stage
as Dad left me there, alone in a chair,
staring out of a dark bay window.

8.

In theory, little bay,
if I bailed this white boat
and rowed out over you,
I could get to Sweden,
the Atlantic, even Canada,
as the Vikings did.

9.

My father had gone to Woolworths,
picked out a pack of stamps –
Africa & Asia Assorted –
handed them to me,
'For your album…'

A man stranded,
my fear reminded him of his.
I sat with the stamps in the back of the car.
He drove us home, circling me
wordlessly with his arms,
the bay I never saw.

Lost

a glove in Chicago

    a belt in Venice

a camera in Beijing

    the angle-poise lamp

        in an Edinburgh taxi

my father's shaving brush

in Graz one October

        a good friend

in Manchester

    passwords

footprints

    that arrow in the snow

Early Warning

squats high
on the school roof
above the pine-tops
like the toy trumpet
of a giant child

its silence holds every blade
of grass, each raindrop
and shoelace and chocolate bar,
every hair, all stories, each
feather, every ear

it squats on the rooftops
against the end and we
are on our little knees
under our desks
giggling

Society

From our boat my cousin
        is pumping pellets
                at a watersnake

    who's trying
         so very hard to flee
                over the flat dark roof
                        of her home

    when she stops
        head full of lead
               he laughs and flips her slinky with an oar

                to shudder

            on my bare feet

My screams I know
can be heard
all along the beach

where everyone
listens and pretends

Our Polar Bear

had disemboweled herself, been to the dentist
for bright acrylic canines, seen the optician for eyes
that would never close in sleep or wind, then
slid spread-eagled, just fur and skin

all the way from Labrador to our place
so O'Connell and me could lie in her warmth
rough like hay on the cool basement floor
on afternoons midweek in midsummer, free

from the heat that baked the sky round
the fatherless houses where wives
pondered sex and supper and gazed
from windows at the listening trees

and fresh-tarred streets laid out in the sun
while we, elbows on that massive head,
her jaws fixed open to receive suburban dust
and the occasional offering of chocolate or chips

underground on our Arctic magic carpet
imagined her flying with us across the great
whiteness beneath the Northern Lights and where
our lives might go after this.

Much later Moshi, half-Inuit teenage babysitter,
down from the North with his English Mum and four sisters
for Education, fell asleep on our window sofa
and couldn't wake till shaken, though we yelled,

told us he'd dreamed how his Dad would take him far
out onto the ice for days teaching him to hunt the Fish, the Seal
and the White Bear, one of which, one warm afternoon,
almost killed them.

Encounter

In the beginning
what did we know of an end?
In church the greying grownups hymned of it
but only with words. Everyone obvious
was still around and along the highway
on the infinite drive to the cottage
twice a year, counting cemeteries
never amounted to anything

till one day
in a dried-up ditch far across
the west field, me and O'Connell
wading dopily through August heat
bumped into it, lounging naked
in a sheep's innermost thoughts
a grinning hum of maggots and flies
under the clear blue sky

Pond

There was a pond not far away
mud-rim pocked with fossil hooves
like a moon its craters
shallowpan tint of rain and cattlepiss
though cows and their owners long gone

Days we drifted a raft grey
barn door hammered on stray
fence-posts upheld by barrels
filled with the caught breath
of pioneers and betrayed animals

O we Huckleberryfinned
through the reeds and cat-tails
gripped poles thrust dark
out of sight, cries scaring
the red-wing blackbirds and us

For we knew
that in that very water
a bargain dwelled, the pond an eye
cold as a star, watching and waiting
for the last of us to stay
the first to wander far

Fifteen

She stood among
the crimson candles
of staghorn sumac
on the strip of shore

between manicured
parkway and river
removed her clothes
item by item and

piled them with care
on a flat rock beside her
neat as correspondence
in an office in-tray.

A breeze flickered
in the leaves, and fields
of goose-bumps blew across
her arms and breasts.

You can't touch she said
*but I wanted you to see
what they're all after
so you won't be confused.*

Her body was so simple
her eyes wide open to me;
I couldn't move or speak
and of course I didn't see.

Catalpa

At home in a jungle, heart-shaped
chest-sized leaves from Rousseau,
exotic for a suburb in a nation
whose faith was banality.
Weird, lush, hungry, and flowers
astonished yellow, it sat on their lawn
sighing under spring rain, limp
in breathless summer, a dancer
in wind, fallen penis seed-pods
hoarded in autumn for our little wars.

Two women lived behind it –
two women together, foreign,
on one blade-edge of porch-step tongues
escaped Jews, on the other Nazi
camp-guards on the run, blinds
drawn, seldom seen, and then so
unsurprising, prodding prim petunias,
mowing and raking the silent grass,
and in winter shovelling snow
from their *Volkswagen* drive.

Why would a tree like that
take root and glory in our dull soil?
Two women, together,
kept themselves to themselves,
lived there all our growing years,
live there still, when
on particular long nights,
I walk back up that street
to beg forgiveness,
naming all the lost names.

At the Bowling Alley

That Saturday morning in spring
unwashed clouds slung low
over the roofs, snow-breath
condensing in the streets and a breeze
still shivering up from the last
river ice.

I'm watching Ray gobble
bacon and fries from a chipped white plate
at the cafe counter, nobody around
just the pock-faced greaser
quiff black and glinting who's serving today.
Behind us the unlit lanes lie soundless.

Ray and I are talking, maybe about records
school, hockey, maybe his sister Susie.
We're together like friends, but
when I reach over to take a fry he snarls & bares
his silver tooth – *That's my breakfast!*
It's almost noon.

Outside at the edges slush flecked with oil
and grit loiters in patches and autumn junk sprouts
from retreating snow but inside a taste in the air
of meat cooked days ago and lasting
all the way from then
to this page.

Now the waiter places his forearms
on the bar, leans close to my face.
I bet you're a GOOD boy, I bet you had Cheerios
and white toast and Mommy's home-made jam hours ago
maybe even pancakes and real maple syrup
not the shit we serve here
you little prick.

That day I learned three things –

1. I was understood to be good
2. People who don't know you can hate you
3. In every head there's something different going on

and there was Ray's faint smile
his silence.

The Telling

November, the world dead
waiting for snow & at dusk
Ray coaxed his sister Susie
to the one-bulb garage where

O'Connell & Ralph plus one
cluster by the open tail-gate
of the family Ford & on it
thirteen she's placed &

in the thick padding
of her winter coat & cords
squirms as they grip
her ankles & wrists

whimpers *I'll tell I'll tell*
while eight hands take
turns to search the places
where the secrets

are meant to hide
O'Connell in the lead
voice his yet not
his hissing in a tongue

untaught but learned
you like it really really
Ray in her ear *don't tell
don't you tell or else* till

they scatter into the night
O'Connell & Ray away
to smoke somewhere
I guess & Ralph plus one

to crouch in the field
behind the house the dark
field all the leaves & weeds
silent & waiting the lovely

snow field the past field
at the edge of its last dark
before the houses & malls
erase it willing nothing

but to forget & pray
Susie, God, or anyone
don't tell don't tell don't tell
They didn't. It's told.

Empire

for Hugh

And over dinner
she told how her pet gazelle,
a gift from the King of Libya,
kept free to graze in the high gardens
of the Fortess of Malta where
her father was commander
of the Mediterranean Fleet,
had one day simply
leapt over the wall
to its death.

Migration

Foxed goose at the mouth of a field by the brambled
wartime bomb-drop, insides-out and flying-gear
splayed for all and the sky to stop and stare –
just the usual shameless strip-tease of death
but for this broadcast of your fabled down
flurrying over the derelict pasture
here at a city's ragged fringe
so white on the green
wind of a spring
afternoon.

No fox
to see of course –
he's denned in the past
and left no easy pickings
for the CSI, only a fox-red dog
downwind, tugging its captive human
towards your body odour.   But you
you're already gone, your soundless ghost
honks away over the autumn river out of sight
like all the other disappeared things, generations.

3. THE WOMEN ARE KNITTING

The Border River

River Finn, Northern Ireland, 2019

Birdsong by the water
I couldn't name
Nor from which side
The birdsong came

It called again
It called again
But from which country
I couldn't name

Walking from Ireland to Ireland

Clady Bridge, County Tyrone, 2019

Crossing this border bridge
among swallows, bearing all
that a head can hold for any distance
and whatever nestles now
in the heart's suitcase.

The river is high today,
some spent storm's afterlife;
cars pass close, obeying
the beat of red-amber-green,
and horses graze in the littered pasture.

Now a boy shouts from the far side
by the village bar that squats so plain
it could be posed in sepia
a century ago, but the boy's shirt
is bright-red.

Every river divides and joins,
and anyone would admit the land
looks the same on both sides.
In a few days you'll grasp
some of what you don't know:
the bar *Kirk's*, the lad Brian,
that used car-lot flogging its deals
on the footprint of an army watchtower.

But now, when the passing stranger,
a regular, turns to ask
Do you have people here?
his gentle way of saying
What are you doing on our bridge?
you claim the easy ignorance of tourists.

Everywhere the world is local,
the sky seamless over all borders
inside and out, those countries
where fear, yearning, swallows
cross from bank to bank carelessly
belonging, or not.

The Women Are Knitting

County Tyrone, 2019

The women are knitting a bridge
With coffee and biscuits offered to strangers
Ordinary women are knitting a bridge

With long twists of rain that fall in the hills
On the slippery banks of meandering peace
The women are knitting a bridge

In kitchens and fields in their woollen shawls
Beside the rivers that course along borders
The women are knitting a bridge

With the ghosts of their grandmothers smuggled from graves
To unravel the yarns that partition the air
Ordinary women are knitting a bridge

If they stop, the fish and children may die
In toxic rushes among watchtower ghosts
Ordinary women are knitting a bridge

In the face of the dark boys carrying death
And twisting tongues that cast off the truth
The women are knitting a bridge
Ordinary women are knitting a bridge

Collage

for Margaret Speak

It was certainly a challenge –
so many miles apart and years
and so scattered –
one in Australia, one
in Canada, and yet another
(who holds my hand)
in the country of the dead.

But nothing fazed Mother –
photos she commanded
from the four winds,
cereal-box card,
a junkshop frame,
scissors, paste,
and here we are, forever.

The family that loves
will always stick together,
she'd say, not without a wink,
not without a distant look.

Lilacs

Lilacs you pronounced *Lie-locks*
and one April day I came from school
arms full of them for you, violet torn
from the fringe of the derelict farm
on the highway going west.

Later you stood alone in our street
where me and my friends fooled
with a basketball, begging me
to the church choir audition,
in tears, in front of mere boys.

O lie-locks! you'd said,
How lovely! trimming and fluffing them
caringly into your best vase
like you'd never seen such in your life
and outside in our yard branches
brimming with their violet.

Woman on a Bridge, Ireland

from a glass plate negative, c. 1910

Already you're out of time, seriously
old-fashioned. Street lads snigger
at your veil, the Sabbath cape donned
on a weekday, that fur muff

from your grave, dead aunt.
Already the century has turned away
from all that seemed briefly true
to leave you stranded half-way

between here and there, where
the cutwater parapets to your left
and right greet and regret
the river's passage,

waves of stone and light looping back
into the past and ahead, beyond your frame,
towards new fads and atrocities
on our side of this window.

Maybe you thought your times
were the best, and you blessed
to be alive, there where the world
seems simpler, black and white.

And maybe you wouldn't have cared
how sharp tongues teased, dressed
in your best on the empty bridge
while the man with the camera

steadied himself above the current –
if only Duffy, ever the limelight hog,
hadn't trundled up in his trap
to complicate the scene.

Yet here he sits, horse and all, hovering
dumbly over your left shoulder forever.
Sure, much better if it had just been you
standing prim in your cape and era

poised between your place and ours
holding the bridge for the whole
feckless village, still, against all those
from beyond the pale –
pagans, sinners, street lads, Duffy, us,
late-comers all.

Garden Buddha

Beneath slow clouds and quick bird-shadow,
by a head-high wall from Victoria's time,
petals bee-laden, pink and mauve in the favoured tints
of real and imagined grandmothers
gossiping beside us in their flowery dresses,
a huge hydrangea holds court, while we sit
with our coffees and iPhones,
disagreeing in the bright morning –
You don't love me.
I love you.

In the glade of their petticoats, rainwash
and pollen, open palms bearing pebbles
brought here from faraway beaches,
a Buddha sits cross-legged. Undisturbed
by bees or birds, the curious cat,
or a distant sky flickering through leaves,
he never looks sideways, up, or out,
but always inwards, sublime and certain,
as may be expected only from the perfect,
and from concrete things.

HPA 515

after Paul Nash, photograph taken near Avebury, 1942

I stopped by the roadside monolith
that stood in the daisies and dust
like a soldier awaiting a lift, on watch,
or both; but although in jest I opened
the passenger door and beckoned
it wouldn't leave its post, go AWOL
to hasten its journey
over the Wiltshire plain.

Things darkened.
How long before stone turns
to cloud, worn out by wandering?
This one to me was a spirit,
its soul sheer depth, timeless, dull,
care-free, complete.

But I picked up my camera,
stepped out into troubled England
walked back down the road
a certain distance, to the very spot
from which you now look,
and pictured the scene –

fences, fields, trees, horizons
all marching away under the sky,
the great dumb gnarled rock decked
in bright lichen, and beside it my little car
driven that day like Apollinaire's
from one age to another,
paused here on the road,
door open, a wish.

Journey

after Paul Nash, 'Dyke by the Road', 1922

The task seemed simple enough –
we cross a stream
bright in winter ice-light,
its waves blades passing
under a guardian tree, then

through a gate that clangs
behind as we head out
over cross-hatched earth
to the house where
we'll live forever.

I see we've just been married –
you wear your wedding veil
and all day I've walked
in my father's shoes
but now they won't fit.
Our hands touch
yet however far we go
the house recedes.

What sort of tryst is this –
the slap of water louder
the air around us
suddenly visible
like time in a museum?

December Wedding, 1942

i.m. Harold and Gladys Powell

So cold the carnation's crimson
stiffens on her black fur coat
up the flight of snow-scraped steps
from the car to the church door
petals bruising to brown
even while the priest intones
a script that binds them
in a way we can't know.

As for the groom, trembling
and shy he can't believe his luck –
the most beautiful girl in town –
though her brother will tease him for years
about the price-tags on his soles
seen as he kneels at the altar
and bought (like the pin-striped suit)
with borrowed money.

Where did they go later?
Nowhere special, not far,
and afterwards, for years
afterwards, they take pride
in not having much,
not wanting much.
They had enough
they believed.

Catch

In the clinic a nurse
says hello, fishes my name
from a deep database,
wishes me barefoot, shirtless –
I lie back in a dim half-sleep.

*

There, my *Klinkhåmer Special*
frets on a river's brown stage,
beneath a proscenium of late summer
oak, cast in the role of water nymph,
a Blue-winged Olive transforming for flight;

and the sting in its tale plays out,
caught in the lip of a teenage trout,
size of a glasses case, slick
as soap, lovely, foolish in air,
caught out.

*

As for foolish, here I am –
a fishing virgin chest-deep
in dizzying water, decked
in rubber, net, straw hat,
skateboarding on an unseen
prehistoric carpet of stone –

a daft impediment in the river's
patient circulation, around
me an everthrown veil
of white flotsam adrift on a flow
going where it's told to go.

*

Writing is fishing,
words sensed flitting
just beyond light
like heart-beats;

and with poor hooks,
half-skill, half-luck,
sightless, line by line,
here we go, casting about.

*

The little trout slips quick
from my wetted fingers
back down through
its bright skylight,

and with practised hands
the nurse fixes small pads,
sky-blue, to my ankles,
wrists, chest,

then stands waiting
for the pulse to appear
on a dull screen,
a signature swimming
in its bed of bone.
*I'll just print this off
then unhook you*, she says.
I do the same with the poem.

Instructions for Counting a River

for Ian Banks

Stir the shallows with waterproof boots till mud-cloudy.
Extract 1 bucket of this whisked water and pour into large tray.
Lift 3 random river stones, fist-sized.
Scrub their skins into the tray.
Return stones to river.

Searching carefully in the tray, exclude extraneous creatures –
the shape-shifting leech,
the writhing water worm,
3 crayfish the size of fingernails,
a Blue-winged Olive that hatches while you watch
(thus absolving itself from the calculation)

Number remaining specimens –
    cased Caddis × 15
    uncased Caddis × 16
    Bullfish × 2
    Stonefly × 20
    Blue-winged Olive × 9
    Olive × 10
    a single Stone-clinging Nymph

List them.
Photograph your list.
Report findings by mobile phone.
Release all creatures and water.
Repack equipment.

Now straighten, look around –
high upstream in a dry Dales June
in the feathery shade of a curtain of ash
by a three-hundred-year-old bridge
of limestone that bakes patiently in the heat,
silent and still, between hills.

The Old Ox Road by the Aura

Finland, 2018

Rags in rushes on a carpet of birch leaves and mud,
plastic flagons knife-hacked for bait-boxes, capsized
beer-cans like billboards advertising civilization to ants.
This was the long way over years from forests,
log-barns and laboured fields, miles into town,
a plodding exchange of few and always-purposed words
for a leaderless choir of hawkers, bawling soldiers,
women dressed in rainbows, cattle slipping
like country bumpkins on shit-slick cobbles
hard as a merchant's heart.

In those days it followed the river like a smaller friend,
an echo of water on land, bending when it bent, accepting
its single-minded direction of travel, occasional outbursts;
and even in the dark he gleaned enough light
for the journey home, coins stashed, slow beast hauling the wagon
laden with night sky, while far away upriver the damped wood stove,
wife, children – Hanna, Kristina, Jyrki, Anneli –
asleep in their deep silence now.
All this gone by on the track through birch trees,
rags, fishermen's junk.

The Horses, Northern Ireland

Three horses, roan, brown, grey,
under elder branches, on a narrow reach
that echoes the river's unrushed swing
between steep banks it's drowned before
and whose shoulders it will surely cry on again,
graze here by black water at high tide,
perfectly innocent and worldly.

On the far side,
another country, car-hiss whispering
through trees with the urgency
of political aides, while in this one
the wordless creatures are eloquent too,
saying something – some thing –
that could so easily be missed.

And you know what it is, you know,
but in speaking it you'd let it go –
dreaming world, soiled Earth,
countries of lies and tears,
where you're alien in all of these places,
but are being told in certain no uncertain terms
to hear and see.

Coastal Moon

Moon, tonight's sea pirates you,
slips a blade under your guard
so brightly darkly bright,
an offer of transformation
shimmering on its screen
like a foetus in ultrasound.

If sea was our first hearing
waves were its first texts;
there's no address quite like theirs
except perhaps the ever-shifting roar
of all things speaking in tongues
to anyone who'll listen –

and rising in our strange rooms
it's all we can do to find the way
among half-familiar things
to catch your kidnapped glimmer
that draws us back to what we knew
and leaves us anywhere, nowhere,
everywhere.

Notes

'Wish', p 11

Butterworth's mother was a singer: he began composing at an early age, and at Oxford developed an interest in traditional folk-song and dance. He was killed in action on the Somme. The poem was inspired by him, but is not about him.

'Firefighters rescue man from river', p. 32

Odd newspaper headlines sometimes inspire poems that have nothing to do with the actual content of their stories. This one is from *The York Press*.

'Journey', p. 69

The word 'tryst' is from Old French *triste*, a hunter's station (*Chambers*).

'Catch', p 71

I'm not a fisherman, to say the least; but the Blue-winged Olive (*Seratella ignita*) is a water-bred insect from the Mayfly family. A 'Klinkhåmer Special' is one of many lures used in dry fly-fishing to imitate the act of the hatched Olive on the water's surface as it prepares for flight.

'Instructions for Counting a River', p 73

The Riverfly Partnership has established an initiative whereby anglers and others can help monitor the health of watercourses in the U.K. by reporting a count of riverfly larvae on a monthly basis.

Acknowledgements

'The Telling' was commended in the National Poetry Competition 2017. 'Testament' won second prize in the Plough Prize short poem competition 2018. 'Our Polar Bear' was shortlisted in the Winchester Festival Poetry Prize 2019 and published in their anthology. 'Bay Window' was shortlisted in the Strokestown Poetry Festival competition 2019 and published in their anthology. 'Canadian Pacific', 'Collage', 'Garden Buddha', and 'Encounter' were published in *Pennine Platform*; 'At The Bowling Alley' and 'Early Warning' appeared in *The North*.

I'm grateful to the Kone Foundation which enabled my two-month stay at the Saari residency in Finland in 2018, where I worked on many of these poems and explored the River Aura. Thanks to Jan-Erik Andersson and Marjo Malin for their collaboration and company during that time. Thanks also to The Finnish Institute in London for supporting my time in Ireland in 2019 as part of a collaboration with Jan-Erik and Irish-American artist Eileen Hutton, and to the Clady Cross-Community Development Association and Earagail Festival.

Finally, my thanks to Julia Deakin for her insightful and meticulous editing.